IMPROVING PROBLEM-SOLVING SKILLS

for ages 9-10

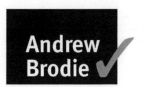

Andrew Brodie ✔

Contents

Andrew Brodie: Improving Problem-solving Skills for ages 9-10 © Bloomsbury Publishing Plc 2013

Introduction

How to use the book and CD-ROM together

The book has fifteen key activities, each opening with an introductory 'context' page to set a scene around which the problem-solving activities are based. The activities are presented on three activity sheets, which can be projected on to a whiteboard for whole class use or photocopied/printed for display. Sharing the activities either on screen or paper provides lots of opportunities for discussing the introductory page and the questions posed, encouraging pupils to use and extend their existing mathematical skills and knowledge.

For each context there are three activity sheets at different ability levels to enable teachers to introduce the problem-solving skills in stages. An animal picture at the top of the sheet indicates the level of the activity sheet. The cat exercises are at the simplest level; the dog exercises are at the next level; the rabbit exercises are at the most advanced level. You may decide to give some pupils the cat activity sheet and then decide, on the basis of their success, to ask them to complete the dog activity sheet. A similar approach could be taken with the dog and rabbit sheets.

The teacher should discuss the tasks, ensuring that the children understand clearly how to enjoy the activity and, where appropriate, how to complete the activity sheet. You may wish to guide the pupils with the 'Steps to Success' shown on page 4.

Answers to all the activity sheets can be found on the CD-ROM.

Talk, talk, talk!

The key to success in solving mathematical problems is understanding the vocabulary of the questions posed. High quality discussion, encouraging the children to consider the context and vocabulary as well as number values, will result in much greater confidence and enthusiasm towards maths.

Some of the questions are inevitably quite wordy and complex. Calm, considered reflection about each context and question will take away the fear and panic that often afflicts children in their approach to the subject.

National Curriculum levels

The activity sheets are aimed at the following ability levels:

- **Cat** activity sheets are for pupils working at Level 3.

- **Dog** activity sheets are for pupils working towards Level 4.

- **Rabbit** activity sheets are for pupils who are working confidently at Level 4.

The Steps to Success

 Step 1: Read the problem carefully and check that you understand it.

 Step 2: Look for key facts and numbers in the question.

 Step 3: Choose the operations you are going to use.

+ − × ÷

 Step 4: Solve the problem and check your answer.

 Step 5: Smile! You have done it!

Andrew Brodie: Improving Problem-solving Skills for ages 9-10 © Bloomsbury Publishing Plc 2013

Comparing numbers

8

23

416

3647

58

23406

697

38119

9

8414

Teacher's notes

Talk about the numbers. Which ones are one-digit numbers? Which ones are two-digit? Which ones are three-digit? Which are four-digit? Which are five-digit? Which ones are odd? Can the children correctly say each number? Do they fully understand the value of each digit in each number? You may like to place the numbers under the column headings: ten thousands; thousands; hundreds; tens and units.
Compare the sizes of the numbers. Add some of the numbers together

Andrew Brodie: Improving Problem-solving Skills for ages 9-10 © Bloomsbury Publishing Plc 2013

Comparing numbers

Look at these numbers.

8	23	3647	
416			58
	38119		
23406			8414
697		9	

Write the one-digit numbers. ☐

Write the two-digit numbers. ☐

Write the three-digit numbers. ☐

Write the four-digit numbers. ☐

Write the five-digit numbers. ☐

Which is the smallest of the numbers? ☐

Which is the biggest of the numbers? ☐

What is the difference between the largest three-digit number and the smallest three-digit number? ☐

Add the three-digit numbers together. ☐

Subtract 416 from 3647. ☐

8414 take away 697. ☐

What is the total of 3647 and 697? ☐

Teacher's notes

Help the children to read the questions, ensuring that they understand the vocabulary – a critical skill in problem-solving. Can they work out what calculations they need to complete?

Name _____

Date _____

Look at the numbers.

8	**23**	**3647**
416	**38119**	**58**
23406	**9**	**8414**
	697	

Write the numbers in order of size, starting with the smallest.

☐	☐	☐	☐	☐
☐	☐	☐	☐	☐

What is the total of 8414 and 416? ☐

What is the difference between 8414 and 3647? ☐

Add 3647 to 8414. ☐

Add the sum of the two-digit numbers to the sum of the
three-digit numbers. ☐

Subtract 3647 from 8414. ☐

Add 8414 to 23406. ☐

Double each of the four-digit numbers. ☐ ☐

Teacher's notes
Help the children to read the questions, ensuring that they understand the vocabulary – a critical skill in problem-solving. Can they work out what calculations they need to complete?

Comparing numbers

Look at the numbers.

8   416   23   3647   58   23406   38119   697   9   8414

Write the numbers in order of size, starting with the smallest.

What is the total of 8414 and 38119?

What is the difference between 38119 and 8414?

Subtract 3647 from 23406.

Multiply 416 by 4.

What is 697 times 7?

Multiply 3647 by 5.

Divide 3647 by 7.

Divide 8414 by 2.

Divide 23406 by 2.

Find the sum of the one-digit, two-digit and three-digit numbers.

What is the total of the four-digit and five-digit numbers?

What is the sum of all the numbers?

Teacher's notes

Help the children to read the questions, ensuring that they understand the vocabulary – a critical skill in problem-solving. Can they work out what calculations they need to complete? The multiplication and division questions may be beyond the scope of the tables the pupils know but can they work out methods to solve them? To answer the final question, do they make use of their previous calculations?

    Andrew Brodie: Improving Problem-solving Skills for ages 9-10 © Bloomsbury Publishing Plc 2013

I think of a number: addition and multiplication

I think of a number. I add 6 then multiply by 2. The answer is 18.

What number did I think of?

I think of a number. I add 4 then multiply by 3. The answer is 33.

What number did I think of

I think of a number. I add 5 then multiply by 4. The answer is 32.

What number did I think of?

I think of a number. I add 7 then multiply by 5. The answer is 45.

What number did I think of?

I think of a number. I add 3 then multiply by 8. The answer is 48.

What number did I think of?

Teacher's notes

Use these examples as a focus for discussion before using the activity sheets, which follow. 'Word problems' such as these can be very challenging for some children: help them to understand the question and encourage them to realize that they have to 'work backwards' – ie to 'undo' an addition they need to subtract, or to 'undo' a multiplication they need to divide. Note also that they will need to take two steps: dividing first then subtracting.

I think of a number: addition and subtraction

I think of a number. I add 3 then multiply by 2. The answer is 14.

What number did I think of?

[ ]

I add 4 then multiply by 6. The answer is 42.

What number did I think of?

[ ]

I think of a number. I add 3 then multiply by 3. The answer is 15.

What number did I think of?

[ ]

I think of a number. I add 3 then multiply by 7. The answer is 63.

What number did I think of?

[ ]

I think of a number. I add 2 then multiply by 4. The answer is 20.

What number did I think of?

[ ]

I think of a number. I add 5 then multiply by 8. The answer is 56.

What number did I think of?

[ ]

I think of a number. I add 6 then multiply by 5. The answer is 40.

What number did I think of?

[ ]

I think of a number. I add 2 then multiply by 9. The answer is 72.

What number did I think of?

[ ]

Teacher's notes

Remind the children that they have to 'work backwards' – ie to 'undo' an addition they need to subtract, or to 'undo' a multiplication they need to divide – and that they will need to take two steps: dividing first then subtracting.

Andrew Brodie: Improving Problem-solving Skills for ages 9-10 © Bloomsbury Publishing Plc 2013

I think of a number: addition and subtraction

I think of a number. I add 3 then multiply by 5. The answer is 40.

What number did I think of?

I think of a number. I add 4 then multiply by 6. The answer is 54.

What number did I think of?

I think of a number. I add 6 then multiply by 8. The answer is 64.

What number did I think of?

I think of a number. I add 12 then multiply by 4. The answer is 100.

What number did I think of?

I think of a number. I add 3 then multiply by 7. The answer is 56.

What number did I think of?

I think of a number. I add 40 then multiply by 4. The answer is 200.

What number did I think of?

I think of a number. I add 7 then multiply by 8. The answer is 96.

What number did I think of?

I think of a number. I add 46 then multiply by 10. The answer is 1000.

What number did I think of?

Teacher's notes
Remind the children that they have to 'work backwards' – ie to 'undo' an addition they need to subtract, or to 'undo' a multiplication they need to divide –w and that they will need to take two steps: dividing first then subtracting.

I think of a number: addition and subtraction

Name _____

Date _____

I think of a number. I add 13 then multiply by 5. The answer is 125.

What number did I think of?

I think of a number. I add 11 then multiply by 6. The answer is 150.

What number did I think of?

I think of a number. I add 16 then multiply by 7. The answer is 140.

What number did I think of?

I think of a number. I add 17 then multiply by 8. The answer is 320.

What number did I think of?

I think of a number. I add 7 then multiply by 9. The answer is 99.

What number did I think of?

I think of a number. I add 25 then multiply by 5. The answer is 400.

What number did I think of?

I think of a number. I add 15 then multiply by 5. The answer is 200.

What number did I think of?

I think of a number. I add 12 then multiply by 9. The answer is 360.

What number did I think of?

Teacher's notes

Remind the children that they have to 'work backwards' – ie to 'undo' an addition they need to subtract, or to 'undo' a multiplication they need to divide – and that they will need to take two steps: dividing first then subtracting.

I think of a number: multiplication and division

I think of a number. I multiply by 2. The answer is 90.

What number did I think of?

I think of a number. I divide by 3. The answer is 42.

What number did I think of?

I think of a number. I divide by 2. The answer is 150.

What number did I think of?

I think of a number. I multiply by 4. The answer is 420.

What number did I think of?

I think of a number. I multiply by 5. The answer is 400.

What number did I think of?

I think of a number. I divide by 4. The answer is 80.

What number did I think of?

I think of a number. I divide by 5. The answer is 60.

What number did I think of?

I think of a number. I multiply by 10. The answer is 2000.

What number did I think of?

I think of a number. I multiply by 3. The answer is 120.

What number did I think of?

I think of a number. I divide by 10. The answer is 150.

What number did I think of?

Teacher's notes

Use these examples as a focus for discussion before using the activity sheets, which follow. 'Word problems' such as these can be very challenging for some children: help them to understand the question and encourage them to realize that they have to 'work backwards' – ie to 'undo' a multiplication they need to divide, or to 'undo' a division they need to multiply.

Name _____

Date _____

I think of a number. I multiply by 2. The answer is 30.

What number did I think of?

I think of a number. I multiply by 5. The answer is 200.

What number did I think of?

I think of a number. I divide by 2. The answer is 18.

What number did I think of?

I think of a number. I divide by 4. The answer is 25.

What number did I think of?

I think of a number. I multiply by 2. The answer is 50.

What number did I think of?

I think of a number. I multiply by 4. The answer is 200.

What number did I think of?

I think of a number. I divide by 2. The answer is 42.

What number did I think of?

I think of a number. I divide by 8. The answer is 20.

What number did I think of?

I think of a number. I multiply by 5. The answer is 100.

What number did I think of?

I think of a number. I multiply by 10. The answer is 3000.

What number did I think of?

Teacher's notes

Help the children to read the word problems and to realize that they have to 'work backwards' – ie to 'undo' a multiplication they need to divide, or to 'undo' a division they need to multiply.

I think of a number: multiplication and division

I think of a number. I multiply by 2. The answer is 120.

What number did I think of?

I think of a number. I multiply by 4. The answer is 1000.

What number did I think of?

I think of a number. I divide by 2. The answer is 75.

What number did I think of?

I think of a number. I divide by 4. The answer is 60.

What number did I think of?

I think of a number. I multiply by 2. The answer is 150.

What number did I think of?

I think of a number. I multiply by 8. The answer is 320.

What number did I think of?

I think of a number. I divide by 2. The answer is 85.

What number did I think of?

I think of a number. I divide by 8. The answer is 60.

What number did I think of?

I think of a number. I multiply by 3. The answer is 99.

What number did I think of?

I think of a number. I multiply by 10. The answer is 9650.

What number did I think of?

Teacher's notes
Remind the children that they have to 'work backwards' – ie to 'undo' a multiplication they need to divide, or to 'undo' a division they need to multiply. Many of the questions concern numbers that extend beyond the scope of the children's multiplication tables - can they use their skills to find methods for solving the problems?

I think of a number: multiplication and division

I think of a number. I multiply by 2. The answer is 650.

What number did I think of?

I think of a number. I multiply by 4. The answer is 1800.

What number did I think of?

I think of a number. I divide by 2. The answer is 847.

What number did I think of?

I think of a number. I divide by 4. The answer is 175.

What number did I think of?

I think of a number. I multiply by 2. The answer is 1700.

What number did I think of?

I think of a number. I multiply by 5. The answer is 2500.

What number did I think of?

I think of a number. I divide by 2. The answer is 2145.

What number did I think of?

I think of a number. I divide by 5. The answer is 195.

What number did I think of?

I think of a number. I multiply by 3. The answer is 630.

What number did I think of?

I think of a number. I multiply by 10. The answer is 42150.

What number did I think of?

Teacher's notes

Remind the children that they have to 'work backwards' – ie to 'undo' a multiplication they need to divide, or to 'undo' a division they need to multiply. Note that many of the questions on this activity sheet deal with numbers beyond the traditional multiplication tables: pupils will need to logic and number skills to find the missing numbers.

Number sequences: addition

13, 16, 19, 22...

36, 44, 52, 60...

25, 50, 75, 100...

18, 25, 32, 39...

28, 32, 36, 40...

69, 72, 75, 78...

Teacher's notes

Ensure that the children understand that a sequence is a set of numbers where each number is made from the previous one by completing a specific operation. In the case of each of the sequences on this activity sheet the operation is the addition of a particular number. Talk about each sequence – good discussion is a very important aspect in improving problem-solving skills. Which sequences contain only odd numbers? Which ones contain only even numbers? Which contain odd and even numbers? What is the link number for each sequence? What number should come next in each sequence?

Andrew Brodie: Improving Problem-solving Skills for ages 9-10 © Bloomsbury Publishing Plc 2013

Number sequences: addition

Look at this sequence of numbers:

31, 34, 37, 40

The first term in the sequence is 31. What number is added to 31 to make 34? ☐

The second term in the sequence is 34. What number is added to 34 to make 37? ☐

The third term in the sequence is 37. What number is added to 37 to make 40? ☐

Add the same number to 40 to find the next term in the sequence. What is it? ☐

Look at this sequence of numbers:

15, 30, 45, 60

The first term in the sequence is 15. What number is added to 15 to make 30? ☐

The second term in the sequence is 30. What number is added to 30 to make 45? ☐

The third term in the sequence is 45. What number is added to 45 to make 60? ☐

Add the same number to 60 to find the next term in the sequence. What is it? ☐

Look at this sequence of numbers:

125, 150, 175, 200

The first term in the sequence is 125. What number is added to 125 to make 150? ☐

The second term in the sequence is 150. What number is added to 150 to make 175? ☐

The third term in the sequence is 175. What number is added to 175 to make 200? ☐

Add the same number to 200 to find the next term in the sequence. What is it? ☐

Teacher's notes

Ensure that the children understand that a sequence is a set of numbers where each number is made from the previous one by completing a specific operation. Check that the pupils are clear that the numbers in the sequences are known as 'terms'. In the case of each of the sequences on this activity sheet the operation is the addition of a particular number. Talk about each sequence – good discussion is a very important aspect in improving problem-solving skills.

Number sequences: addition

Name _____

Date _____

Look at this sequence of numbers:

68, 76, 84, 92

What is the first term in the sequence? ☐

What operation acts upon each term to find the next term in the sequence? ☐

What would be the fifth term in the sequence? ☐

Look at this sequence of numbers:

97, 103, 109, 115

What is the third term in the sequence? ☐

What operation acts upon each term to find the next term in the sequence? ☐

What would be the fifth term in the sequence? ☐

Look at this sequence of numbers:

45, 90, 135, 180

What is the fourth term in the sequence? ☐

What operation acts upon each term to find the next term in the sequence? ☐

What would be the fifth term in the sequence? ☐

Continue the sequence to answer this question: What is the tenth term in the sequence?

Teacher's notes

Ensure that the children understand that a sequence is a set of numbers where each number is made from the previous one by completing a specific operation. Check that the pupils are clear that the numbers in the sequences are known as 'terms'. In the case of each of the sequences on this activity sheet the operation is the addition of a particular number. Talk about each sequence - good discussion is a very important aspect in improving problem-solving skills.

Andrew Brodie: Improving Problem-solving Skills for ages 9-10 © Bloomsbury Publishing Plc 2013

Name _____

Date _____

Look at this sequence of numbers:

41, 48, 55, 62

Find the next four terms in the sequence.

☐ ☐ ☐ ☐

What would be the tenth term in the sequence?

☐

Look at this sequence of numbers:

39, 47, 55, 63

Find the next four terms in the sequence.

☐ ☐ ☐ ☐

What would be the tenth term in the sequence?

☐

Look at this sequence of numbers:

100, 170, 240, 310

Find the next four terms in the sequence.

☐ ☐ ☐ ☐

What would be the tenth term in the sequence?

☐

Look at this sequence of numbers:

250, 500, 750, 1000

Find the next four terms in the sequence.

☐ ☐ ☐ ☐

What would be the fifteenth term in the sequence?

☐

Teacher's notes

Ensure that the children understand that a sequence is a set of numbers where each number is made from the previous one by completing a specific operation. Check that the pupils are clear that the numbers in the sequences are known as 'terms'. In the case of each of the sequences on this activity sheet the operation is the addition of a particular number. Talk about each sequence – good discussion is a very important aspect in improving problem-solving skills.

Number sequences: subtraction

61, 57, 53, 49...

72, 64, 56, 48...

50, 47, 44, 41...

81, 72, 63, 54...

500, 450, 400, 350...

1000, 975, 950, 925...

Teacher's notes

Ensure that the children understand that a sequence is a set of numbers where each term is made from the previous one by completing a specific operation. In the case of each of the sequences on this activity sheet the operation is the subtraction of a particular number. Talk about each sequence – good discussion is a very important aspect in improving problem-solving skills. Which sequence contains only odd numbers? Which ones contain only even numbers? Which contain odd and even numbers? What is the link number for each sequence? What number should come next in each sequence?

Andrew Brodie: Improving Problem-solving Skills for ages 9-10 © Bloomsbury Publishing Plc 2013

Number sequences: subtraction

Name _____

Date _____

Look at this sequence of numbers:

49, 42, 35, 28

The first term in the sequence is 49. What number is subtracted from 49 to make 42? ☐

The second term in the sequence is 42. What number is subtracted from 42 to make 35? ☐

The third term in the sequence is 35. What number is subtracted from 35 to make 28? ☐

Subtract the same number from 28 to find the next term in the sequence. What is it? ☐

Look at this sequence of numbers:

900, 820, 740, 660

The first term in the sequence is 900. What number is subtracted from 900 to make 820? ☐

The second term in the sequence is 820. What number is subtracted from 820 to make 740? ☐

The third term in the sequence is 740. What number is subtracted from 740 to make 660? ☐

Subtract the same number from 660 to find the next term in the sequence. What is it? ☐

Look at this sequence of numbers:

400, 350, 300, 250

The first term in the sequence is 400. What number is subtracted from 400 to make 350? ☐

The second term in the sequence is 350. What number is subtracted from 350 to make 300? ☐

The third term in the sequence is 300. What number is subtracted from 300 to make 250? ☐

Subtract the same number from 250 to find the next term in the sequence. What is it? ☐

Teacher's notes

Ensure that the children understand that a sequence is a set of numbers where each number is made from the previous one by completing a specific operation. Check that the pupils are clear that the numbers in the sequences are known as 'terms'. In the case of each of the sequences on this activity sheet the operation is the subtraction of a particular number. Talk about each sequence – good discussion is a very important aspect in improving problem-solving skills.

Andrew Brodie: Improving Problem-solving Skills for ages 9-10 © Bloomsbury Publishing Plc 2013

Number sequences: subtraction

Name _____

Date _____

Look at this sequence of numbers:

10000, 9300, 8600, 7900

What is the first term in the sequence? ☐

What operation acts upon each term to find the next term in the sequence? ☐

What would be the fifth term in the sequence? ☐

Look at this sequence of numbers:

6200, 5800, 5400, 5000

What is the third term in the sequence? ☐

What operation acts upon each term to find the next term in the sequence? ☐

What would be the fifth term in the sequence? ☐

Look at this sequence of numbers:

625, 580, 535, 490

What is the fourth term in the sequence? ☐

What operation acts upon each term to find the next term in the sequence? ☐

What would be the fifth term in the sequence? ☐

Continue the sequence to answer this question: What is the tenth term in the sequence? ☐

Teacher's notes
Ensure that the children understand that a sequence is a set of numbers where each number is made from the previous one by completing a specific operation. Check that the pupils are clear that the numbers in the sequences are known as 'terms'. In the case of each of the sequences on this activity sheet the operation is the subtraction of a particular number. Talk about each sequence – good discussion is a very important aspect in improving problem-solving skills.

Name _____

Date _____

Look at this sequence of numbers:

10000, 9700, 9400, 9100

Find the next four terms in the sequence.

☐ ☐ ☐ ☐

What would be the tenth term in the sequence?

☐

Look at this sequence of numbers:

4200, 3800, 3400, 3000

Find the next four terms in the sequence.

☐ ☐ ☐ ☐

What would be the tenth term in the sequence?

☐

Look at this sequence of numbers:

3200, 2950, 2700, 2450

Find the next four terms in the sequence.

☐ ☐ ☐ ☐

What would be the tenth term in the sequence?

☐

Look at this sequence of numbers:

12000, 11200, 10400, 9600

Find the next four terms in the sequence.

☐ ☐ ☐ ☐

What would be the fifteenth term in the sequence?

☐

Teacher's notes
Ensure that the children understand that a sequence is a set of numbers where each number is made from the previous one by completing a specific operation. Check that the pupils are clear that the numbers in the sequences are known as 'terms'. In the case of each of the sequences on this activity sheet the operation is the subtraction of a particular number. Talk about each sequence – good discussion is a very important aspect in improving problem-solving skills.

Andrew Brodie: Improving Problem-solving Skills for ages 9-10 © Bloomsbury Publishing Plc 2013

Times of day

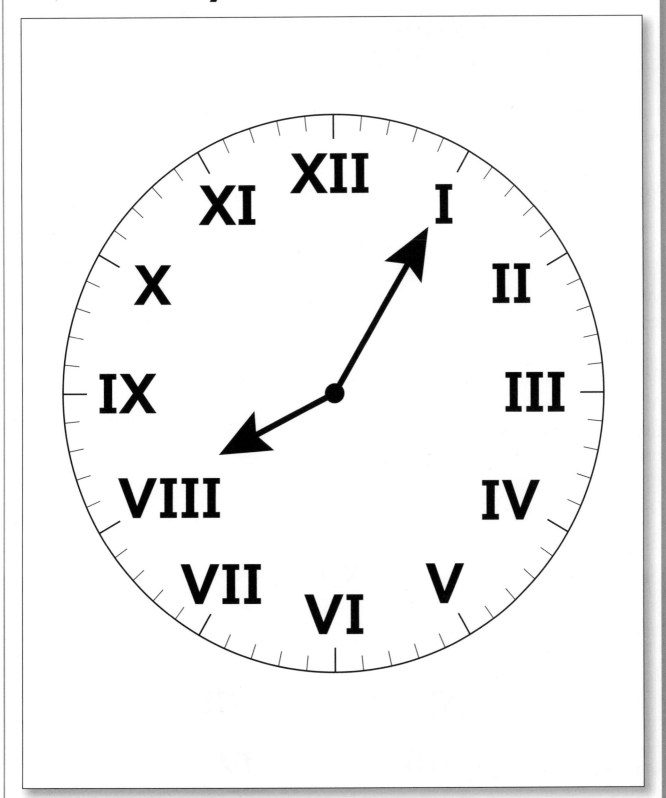

Times of day

Name _____

Date _____

I leave home at 8.35am. It takes me 15 minutes to walk to school.
At what time do I arrive at school?

We go to assembly at 9.05am. How long after I reach school is this?

Assembly lasts for 20 minutes. At what time does it finish?

We then have maths, which lasts until break time. Break time
starts at 10.30am. How long is the maths lesson?

Break time is twenty minutes long. What time does break finish?

Lunch time starts at 12.15pm. How long is the session from
break until lunch time?

Draw hands on the clock face to show the time 23 minutes past 11.

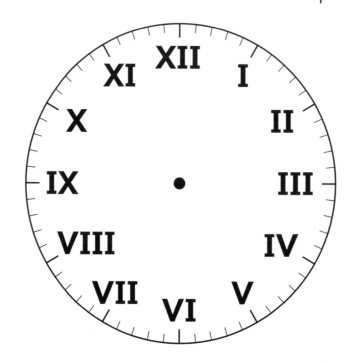

Teacher's notes

Ensure that the pupils have thoroughly discussed the clock on the context page. Help them to read and interpret
the questions on this page and encourage them to write answers in an appropriate format for time.

Andrew Brodie: Improving Problem-solving Skills for ages 9-10 © Bloomsbury Publishing Plc 2013

Jasmine gets up at 7.25am.

School starts at 8.55am. How long is this after Jasmine gets up?

Break time starts an hour and a half after the start of the school day. At what time does break start?

Break lasts for 20 minutes then there is an hour and a half until lunch time. What time does the lunch break start?

Lunch break has a length of 55 minutes. At what time does the afternoon session start?

School finishes at 3.15pm. How long is the afternoon session?

It takes Jasmine 20 minutes to get home after school. What time does she get home?

Jasmine has tea at 5.15pm. How long is this after she gets home?

Jasmine goes to bed at 8.30pm. How long is this after she gets in from school?

How long is this after she gets up in the morning?

Teacher's notes

Ensure that the pupils have thoroughly discussed the clock on the context page. Help them to read and interpret the questions on this page and encourage them to write answers in an appropriate format for time.

Times of day

The table shows the timetable of Jasmine's day. The times are shown in 12-hour clock format and in 24-hour clock format. Fill in the missing data.

Activity	12-hour clock time	24-hour clock time
Jasmine gets up	7.25am	0725
School starts	8.55am	
Break starts	10.25am	
Break finishes	10.45am	
Lunch break starts	12.15pm	
Lunch break finishes	1.10pm	
School finishes		1515
Jasmine gets home		1535
Tea time starts	5.15pm	
Bed time	8.30pm	

How long after the start of school does lunch break start? Give your answer in hours and minutes.

[ ] hours [ ] minutes

Now give the answer in minutes.

[ ] minutes

How long after lunch finishes does school finish for the day? Give your answer in hours and minutes.

[ ] hours [ ] minutes

Now give the answer in minutes.

[ ] minutes

How long after the start of school in the morning does school finish at the end of the day? Give your answer in hours and minutes.

[ ] hours [ ] minutes

Now give the answer in minutes.

[ ] minutes

Taking out time for the two breaks, how long is the school day? Give your answer in hours and minutes.

[ ] hours [ ] minutes

Now give the answer in minutes.

[ ] minutes

Teacher's notes

Ensure that the pupils have thoroughly discussed the clock on the context page. Help them to read and interpret the questions on this page and encourage them to write answers in an appropriate format for time.

Andrew Brodie: Improving Problem-solving Skills for ages 9-10 © Bloomsbury Publishing Plc 2013

Clothing materials

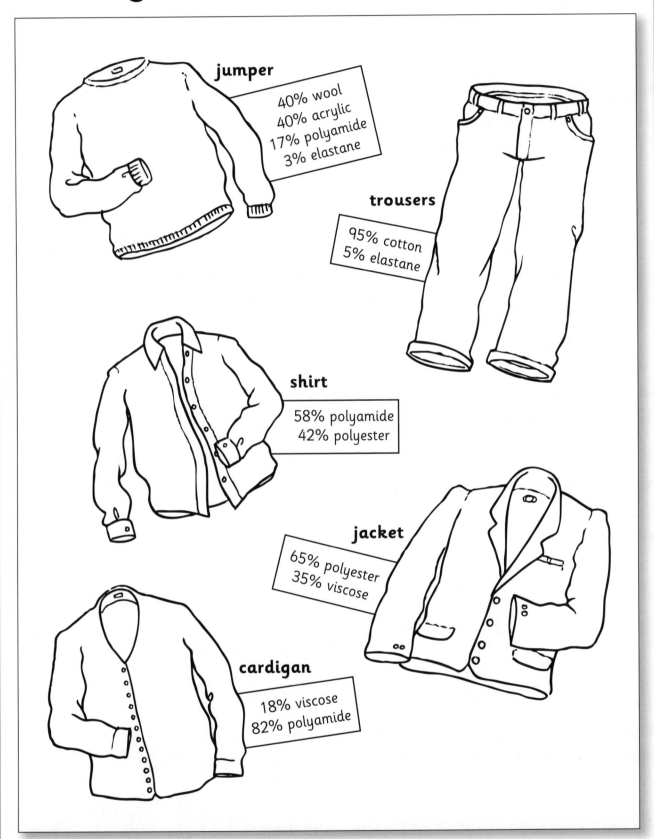

jumper

40% wool
40% acrylic
17% polyamide
3% elastane

trousers

95% cotton
5% elastane

shirt

58% polyamide
42% polyester

jacket

65% polyester
35% viscose

cardigan

18% viscose
82% polyamide

Teacher's notes

Discuss the clothes labels. Ask the pupils to find the total of all the materials for each item of clothing, encouraging them to notice that it is always 100. Are they aware that percentages are always related to a total of 100?

Name _____

Date _____

Clothing materials

The material of a jumper is shown on the label as 82% wool and the rest is polyester.
What percentage is polyester?

[ ]

The material of a pair of trousers is shown on the label as 76% cotton and the rest is polyester.
What percentage is polyester?

[ ]

The material of a cardigan is shown on the label as 87% polyamide and the rest is viscose.
What percentage is viscose?

[ ]

Another cardigan is made of viscose and linen.
The percentage of linen is 55%.
What is the percentage of viscose?

[ ]

A jacket is made of 35% viscose and the rest is polyester.
What percentage is polyester?

[ ]

A shirt is made of polyamide and and polyester.
The percentage of polyester is 39%.
What percentage is polyamide?

[ ]

If a shirt was made of cotton and viscose and the percentage of viscose was 32%,
what percentage would the cotton be?

[ ]

Teacher's notes
Remind the pupils that percentages are always related to a total of 100.

Andrew Brodie: Improving Problem-solving Skills for ages 9-10 © Bloomsbury Publishing Plc 2013

Clothing materials

The material of a jumper is shown on the label as 76% wool and the rest is polyester. What percentage is polyester?

The material of a pair of trousers is shown on the label as 58% cotton and the rest is polyester. What percentage is polyester?

The material of a cardigan is shown on the label as 46% cotton, 28% acrylic and the rest is lycra. What percentage is lycra?

A jumper is made from material consisting of polyamide together with 35% wool, 49% acrylic and 2% elastane. What percentage of the material is polyamide?

A shirt is made from 46% cotton, together with polyester and polyamide in equal proportions. What is the percentage for polyester and polyamide?

Another shirt is made from 58% cotton, together with polyester and polyamide in equal proportions. What is the percentage for polyester and polyamide?

A jacket is made from 4% elastane, together with wool, acrylic and polyamide in equal proportions. What is the percentage for wool, acrylic and polyamide?

wool   acrylic   polyamide

Teacher's notes

Remind the pupils that percentages are always related to a total of 100.

Name _____

Date _____

A jumper is made from material consisting of polyamide together with 42% wool, 34% acrylic and 6% elastane. What percentage of the material is polyamide?

A shirt is made from 68% cotton, together with polyester and polyamide in equal proportions. What is the percentage for polyester and polyamide?

Another shirt is made from 36% cotton, together with polyester and polyamide in equal proportions. What is the percentage for polyester and polyamide?

A jacket is made from 7% elastane, together with wool, acrylic and polyamide in equal proportions. What is the percentage for wool, acrylic and polyamide?

A cardigan is made from 48% polyamide, together with wool and acrylic. There is three times as much wool as acrylic. What is the percentage of wool?

What is the percentage of acrylic?

Another jacket is made from polyester, viscose and elastane. The percentage of elastane is a quarter of the percentage of viscose. The combined percentage of elastane and viscose is a quarter of the total material. Find the percentage of each material.

☐ polyester ☐ viscose ☐ elastane

Teacher's notes
Remind the pupils that percentages are always related to a total of 100. The final two questions are particularly challenging!

Calendar

2015 Calendar

January

Su	M	Tu	W	Th	F	Sa
				1	2	3
4	5	6	7	8	9	10
11	12	13	14	15	16	17
18	19	20	21	22	23	24
25	26	27	28	29	30	31

February

Su	M	Tu	W	Th	F	Sa
1	2	3	4	5	6	7
8	9	10	11	12	13	14
15	16	17	18	19	20	21
22	23	24	25	26	27	28

March

Su	M	Tu	W	Th	F	Sa
1	2	3	4	5	6	7
8	9	10	11	12	13	14
15	16	17	18	19	20	21
22	23	24	25	26	27	28
29	30	31				

April

Su	M	Tu	W	Th	F	Sa
			1	2	3	4
5	6	7	8	9	10	11
12	13	14	15	16	17	18
19	20	21	22	23	24	25
26	27	28	29	30		

May

Su	M	Tu	W	Th	F	Sa
					1	2
3	4	5	6	7	8	9
10	11	12	13	14	15	16
17	18	19	20	21	22	23
24	25	26	27	28	29	30
31						

June

Su	M	Tu	W	Th	F	Sa
	1	2	3	4	5	6
7	8	9	10	11	12	13
14	15	16	17	18	19	20
21	22	23	24	25	26	27
28	29	30				

July

Su	M	Tu	W	Th	F	Sa
			1	2	3	4
5	6	7	8	9	10	11
12	13	14	15	16	17	18
19	20	21	22	23	24	25
26	27	28	29	30	31	

August

Su	M	Tu	W	Th	F	Sa
						1
2	3	4	5	6	7	8
9	10	11	12	13	14	15
16	17	18	19	20	21	22
23	24	25	26	27	28	29
30	31					

September

Su	M	Tu	W	Th	F	Sa
		1	2	3	4	5
6	7	8	9	10	11	12
13	14	15	16	17	18	19
20	21	22	23	24	25	26
27	28	29	30			

October

Su	M	Tu	W	Th	F	Sa
				1	2	3
4	5	6	7	8	9	10
11	12	13	14	15	16	17
18	19	20	21	22	23	24
25	26	27	28	29	30	31

November

Su	M	Tu	W	Th	F	Sa
1	2	3	4	5	6	7
8	9	10	11	12	13	14
15	16	17	18	19	20	21
22	23	24	25	26	27	28
29	30					

December

Su	M	Tu	W	Th	F	Sa
		1	2	3	4	5
6	7	8	9	10	11	12
13	14	15	16	17	18	19
20	21	22	23	24	25	26
27	28	29	30	31		

Teacher's notes

Talk about the calendar for 2015. Depending on when you use this activity you may need to discuss the calendar in terms of a future year, the present year or a year in the past! What day of the week is the first day of the year shown? What day of the week is the last day of the year? What day of the week was the last day of the previous year? How many days are there in each month? How many weeks and days are there in each month? The activities on the activity sheet pages cover different mathematical skills to those on the calendar pages of *Improving Problem-solving Skills for ages 8-9* – you may like to revise those pages with the pupils first.

Calendar

Look at the calendar for 2015.

Find out the dates of the birthdays of children in your class. Draw a ring around each date on the 2015 calendar.

Use the data to complete the table below.

Number of children in the class with a birthday on a...	Tally of results	Total number
Monday		
Tuesday		
Wednesday		
Thursday		
Friday		
Saturday		
Sunday		

Which day of the week has the highest number of birthdays?

Which day of the week has the least number of birthdays?

Teacher's notes

Issue the pupils with a copy of the calendar for 2015 to enable them to gather data about everyone in the class. Talk about the task, ensuring that the pupils understand what they have to do.

Andrew Brodie: Improving Problem-solving Skills for ages 9-10 © Bloomsbury Publishing Plc 2013

Calendar

Look at the calendar for 2015.

Find out the dates of the birthdays of people in your class. Draw a ring around each date on the 2015 calendar.

Use the data to complete the table below.

Number of children in the class with a birthday in...	Tally of results	Total number
January		
February		
March		
April		
May		
June		
July		
August		
September		
October		
November		
December		

Which month has the highest number of birthdays?

Which month has the least number of birthdays?

Teacher's notes

Issue the pupils with a copy of the calendar for 2015 to enable them to gather data about everyone in the class. Talk about the task, ensuring that the pupils understand what they have to do.

Calendar

Name _____

Date _____

Look at the calendar for 2015.

Find out the dates of the birthdays of all members of your class. On the grid below create an appropriate bar chart showing the number of birthdays in each month.

Teacher's notes

Issue the pupils with a copy of the calendar for 2015 to enable them to gather data about everyone in the class. Talk about the task, ensuring that the pupils understand what they have to do. The problem-solving skills required here are not only concerned with gathering data but also how to set that data out: the pupils need to make their own decisions regarding calibration of their chart, which axis to use for frequency and which to use for the months. Encourage them to examine their own work critically: is the data set out clearly enough?

Andrew Brodie: Improving Problem-solving Skills for ages 9-10 © Bloomsbury Publishing Plc 2013

Group photo

Simon
1m 98cm

Emma
1m 59cm

Priti
1m 64cm

Sandeep
1m 76cm

Jess
84cm

Will
1m 2cm

Jas
1m 23cm

Ben
97cm

Teacher's notes

Remind the pupils that m and cm are abbreviations for metre and centimetre. Talk about the word centimetre, pointing out that it has the prefix centi, which means one hundredth. Can they think of other words that start with cent? Encourage them to notice that most of them are related to a hundred.

Group photo

Who is the shortest adult?

What is their height in metres and centimetres?

[   ] m [   ] cm

What is their height just in centimetres?

[   ] cm

What is their height just in metres?

[   ] m

Who is the tallest adult?

What is their height in metres and centimetres?

[   ] m [   ] cm

What is their height just in centimetres?

[   ] cm

What is their height just in metres?

[   ] m

Who is the shortest child?

What is their height in metres and centimetres?

[   ] m [   ] cm

What is their height just in centimetres?

[   ] cm

What is their height just in metres?

[   ] m

How much taller than Ben is Emma? Give your answer in centimetres.

[   ] cm

Now give your answer in metres.

[   ] m

How much shorter than Will is Jess? Give your answer in centimetres.

[   ] cm

Now give your answer in metres.

[   ] m

Teacher's notes

Remind the pupils that m and cm are abbreviations for metre and centimetre. Ensure that they remember that there are 100cm in 1m. The pupils need to show their answers to the first few questions in three different formats: for example, I metre and 8 centimetres could be shown as 1m 8cm, 108cm or 1.08m.

Andrew Brodie: Improving Problem-solving Skills for ages 9-10 © Bloomsbury Publishing Plc 2013

Group photo

Complete the table showing the heights of each person.

Person	Height in metres and centimetres	Height in centimetres	Height in metres
Simon	1m 98 cm		1.98m

Write the names of the people in order of height, starting with the shortest person.

1. [_____] 4. [_____] 7. [_____]

2. [_____] 5. [_____] 8. [_____]

3. [_____] 6. [_____]

How much taller than Will is Priti?
Give your answer in centimetres.

[_____] cm

Now give your answer in metres.

[_____] m

How much shorter than Sandeep is Jas?
Give your answer in centimetres.

[_____] cm

Now give your answer in metres.

[_____] m

How much taller than Jas is Simon?
Give your answer in centimetres.

[_____] cm

Now give your answer in metres.

[_____] m

How much shorter than Emma is Ben?
Give your answer in centimetres.

[_____] cm

Now give your answer in metres.

[_____] m

Teacher's notes
Remind the pupils that m and cm are abbreviations for metre and centimetre. Ensure that they remember that there are 100cm in 1m. The pupils need to complete the heights in the table in three different formats: for example, I metre and 8 centimetres would be shown as 1m 8cm, 108cm or 1.08m.

Group photo

Name _____

Date _____

Complete the table showing the heights of each person.

Person	Height in metres and centimetres	Height in centimetres	Height in metres
Simon	1m 98 cm		1.98m

What is the range of the heights of the adults? Give your answer in centimetres.

[ ] cm

What is the range of the heights of the children? Give your answer in centimetres.

[ ] cm

What is the range of the heights of all the people in the group? Give your answer in centimetres.

[ ] cm

Quick investigation
Give your answers in centimetres.

Measure your arm from the elbow to the tip of your longest finger.

[ ] cm

Measure your leg from your knee to the floor.

[ ] cm

How do the two measurements compare?

[ ] cm

Are your results similar to your friend's?

[ ]

Teacher's notes

The pupils need to complete the heights in the table in four different formats: for example, 1 metre and 8 centimetres would be shown as 1m 8cm, 108cm, 1.08m or 1080mm. Encourage the children to make valid comparisons when completing the quick investigation: are the measurements the same or is one longer than the other? Do the friend's measurements compare in a similar way?

The 400 metre race track

Teacher's notes

Remind the pupils that km and m are abbreviations for kilometre and metre. Talk about the word kilometre, pointing out that it has the prefix kilo, which represents one thousand. Can they think of other words that start with kilo? They may think of kilogram, which is 1000 grams. Can they express 400m as a measurement in kilometres: ie 0.4km?

The 400 metre race track

The race track is a 400m circuit.

Pete runs around the race track twice. How far does he run, in metres?

[ ] m

Give your answer in kilometres.

[ ] km

Anne runs around the race track five times. How far does she run, in metres?

[ ] m

Give your answer in kilometres.

[ ] km

How much further did Anne run than Pete? Give your answer in metres.

[ ] m

Give your answer in kilometres.

[ ] km

Eliza runs around the race track eight times. How far does she run, in metres.

[ ] m

Give your answer in kilometres.

[ ] km

How much further did Eliza run than Pete? Give your answer in metres.

[ ] m

Give your answer in kilometres.

[ ] km

Tariq runs around the race track two and a half times. How far does he run, in metres?

[ ] m

Give your answer in kilometres.

[ ] km

What distance in metres is equal to three and a quarter times round the track?

[ ] m

Now give your answer in kilometres.

[ ] km

Teacher's notes

Remind the pupils that km and m are abbreviations for kilometre and metre. Ensure that they show conversions appropriately, eg 400m = 0.4km; 1200m = 1.2km.

The 400 metre race track

Name _____

Date _____

The race track is a 400m circuit.

What distance in metres is equal to two and a quarter times round the track?

[ ] m

Give your answer in kilometres.

[ ] km

What distance in metres is equal to six and a quarter times round the track?

[ ] m

Give your answer in kilometres.

[ ] km

What distance in metres is equal to eight and three quarters times round the track?

[ ] m

Give your answer in kilometres.

[ ] km

How many times would I need to run round the track to cover a distance of exactly 4km?

[ ] times

How many times would I need to run round the track to cover a distance of exactly 1km?

[ ] times

How many times would I need to run round the track to cover a distance of exactly 2km?

[ ] times

How many times would I need to run round the track to cover a distance of exactly 8km?

[ ] times

How many times would I need to run round the track to cover a distance of exactly 1.5km?

[ ] times

How many times would I need to run round the track to cover a distance of exactly 3.5km?

[ ] times

Teacher's notes

Remind the pupils that km and m are abbreviations for kilometre and metre. Ensure that they show conversions appropriately, eg 400m = 0.4km; 1200m = 1.2km.

The 400 metre race track

Name _____

Date _____

The race track is a 400m circuit.

What distance in metres is equal to four and three quarters times round the track? ☐ m

Give your answer in kilometres. ☐ km

How many times would I need to run round the track to cover a distance of exactly 7km?

☐ times

How many times would I need to run round the track to cover a distance of exactly 10km?

☐ times

How many times would I need to run round the track to cover a distance of exactly 2.5km?

☐ times

George, an athlete, takes an average of 1 minute 55 seconds to run the 400m circuit when he runs round it 6 times.

How far has George run in metres? ☐ m

How far has George run in kilometres? ☐ km

How long did it take George to run the six laps? Give your answer in seconds. ☐ seconds

Now give your answer in minutes and seconds.

☐ minutes ☐ seconds

If George could keep the same average time per lap, how long would it take him to run 4km on the track? Give your answer in seconds. ☐ seconds

Now give your answer in minutes and seconds.

☐ minutes ☐ seconds

Teacher's notes

Remind the pupils that km and m are abbreviations for kilometre and metre. Ensure that they show conversions appropriately, eg 400m = 0.4km; 1200m = 1.2km. The last few questions are very challenging - encourage the pupil to follow logical steps in solving the problems.

Andrew Brodie: Improving Problem-solving Skills for ages 9-10 © Bloomsbury Publishing Plc 2013

Road race

The runners are competing in a road race, over a distance of 9km.

Teacher's notes

Remind the pupils that km and m are abbreviations for kilometre and metre. Talk about the word kilometre, revising the fact that it has the prefix kilo, which represents one thousand. The race is over a distance of 9km - how many metres is this? How many metres would half of this distance be? How many metres would a quarter of the distance be? Three quarters? One tenth? Three tenths? If a runner has run 3.4km, how much further has she got to go? If a runner has run 2.65km, how much further has he got to go?

Road race

The runners are competing in a road race, over a distance of 9km.

How long is the race in metres? ☐ m

How far, in metres, is half the race distance? ☐ m

How many metres is one tenth of the distance? ☐ m

How many metres is three tenths of the distance? ☐ m

How far is seven tenths of the distance? ☐ m

Sally has run 1.2km, how much further does she still have to run?

☐

Jim has run 3.7km, how much further does he still have to run?

☐

Grace has run 6.9km, how much further does she still have to run?

☐

Tariq has run 7.4km, how much further does he still have to run?

☐

Teacher's notes

Ensure that the pupils are clear that 9km is equal to 9000m. Discuss the questions with them. You may like to extend the activity by asking the pupils to convert the answers to the last four questions to metres.

Andrew Brodie: Improving Problem-solving Skills for ages 9-10 © Bloomsbury Publishing Plc 2013

Road race

The runners are competing in a road race, over a distance of 9km.

How long is the race in metres?

[ ] m

How far, in metres, is half the race distance?

[ ] m

How many metres is one quarter of the distance?

[ ] m

How many metres is three quarters of the distance?

[ ] m

How far is three tenths of the distance?

[ ] m

How far is nine tenths of the distance?

[ ] m

Tom has run 3.25km, how much further does he still have to run?

[ ]

Gemma has run 4.67km, how much further does she still have to run?

[ ]

Rob has run 5.92km, how much further does he still have to run?

[ ]

Jasdeep has run 6.78km, how much further does she still have to run?

[ ]

Teacher's notes

Ensure that the pupils are clear that 9km is equal to 9000m. Discuss the questions with them. You may like to extend the activity by asking the pupils to convert the answers to the last four questions to metres.

Road race

The runners are competing in a road race, over a distance of 9km.

How many metres is one quarter of the distance? [ ] m

How many metres is three quarters of the distance? [ ] m

How far is one eighth of the distance? [ ] m

How far is three eighths of the distance? [ ] m

How far is five eighths of the distance? [ ] m

How far is seven eighths of the distance? [ ] m

Will has run 1.795km, how much further does he still have to run?

[ ]

Georgia has run 3.428km, how much further does she still have to run?

[ ]

Ollie has run 6.373km, how much further does he still have to run?

[ ]

Natalie has run 7.005km, how much further does she still have to run?

[ ]

Teacher's notes

Ensure that the pupils are clear that 9km is equal to 9000m. Discuss the questions with them. You may like to extend the activity by asking the pupils to convert the answers to the last four questions to metres.

Andrew Brodie: Improving Problem-solving Skills for ages 9-10 © Bloomsbury Publishing Plc 2013

Squares and rectangles

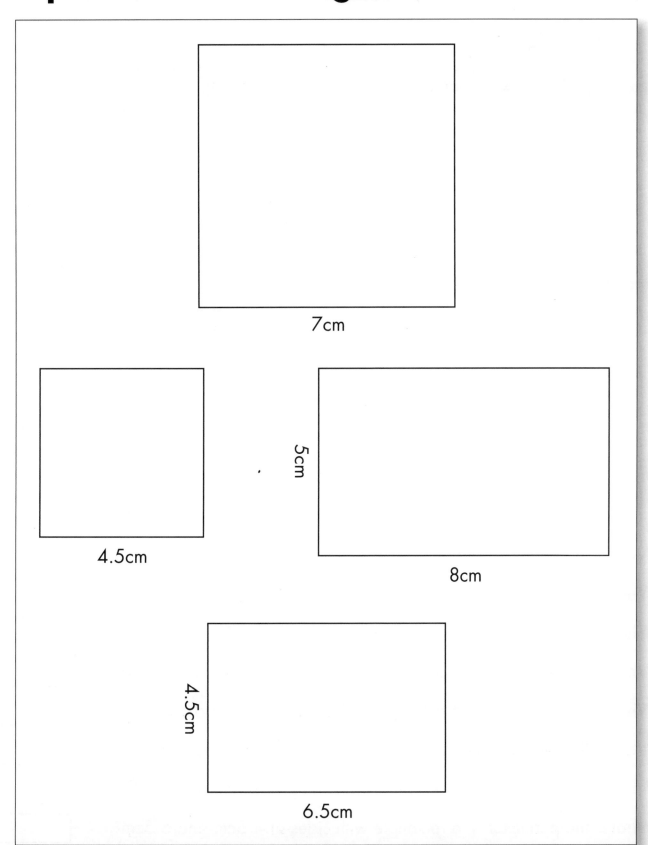

7cm

4.5cm

5cm

8cm

4.5cm

6.5cm

Teacher's notes

Discuss the four shapes shown. Ensure that the pupils understand that the perimeter is the total distance around a shape. Can they find the perimeter of each of the shapes shown?

Andrew Brodie: Improving Problem-solving Skills for ages 9-10 © Bloomsbury Publishing Plc 2013

Name _____

Date _____

Find the perimeter of the square.

3.5cm

Find the perimeter of the rectangle.

2.4cm

6.2cm

What is the perimeter of a square with sides of 4cm?

What is the perimeter of a square with sides of 8cm?

What is the perimeter of a square with sides of 2.5cm?

What is the perimeter of a square with sides of 6.5cm?

What is the perimeter of a rectangle with sides of 7cm and 4cm?

What is the perimeter of a rectangle with sides of 6cm and 5cm?

What is the perimeter of a rectangle with sides of 3.5cm and 2.5cm?

What is the perimeter of a rectangle with sides of 4.5cm and 6.5cm?

Teacher's notes

Ensure that the pupils understand that the perimeter is the total distance around a shape. Can they find the perimeter of each of the shapes shown? Finding the perimeters from the descriptions can be more of a challenge.

Andrew Brodie: Improving Problem-solving Skills for ages 9-10 © Bloomsbury Publishing Plc 2013

Name _____

Date _____

Find the perimeter of the square.

3.5cm

Find the perimeter of the rectangle.

2.4cm

6.2cm

What is the perimeter of a square with sides of 3.2cm?

What is the perimeter of a square with sides of 4.8cm?

What is the perimeter of a square with sides of 5.7cm?

What is the perimeter of a square with sides of 6.9cm?

What is the perimeter of a rectangle with sides of 7.3cm and 2.4cm?

What is the perimeter of a rectangle with sides of 4.7cm and 5.3cm?

What is the perimeter of a rectangle with sides of 6.8cm and 9.2cm?

What is the perimeter of a rectangle with sides of 3.6cm and 4.9cm?

Give your answer to the last question in millimetres.

Teacher's notes

Ensure that the pupils understand that the perimeter is the total distance around a shape. Can they find the perimeter of each of the shapes shown? Finding the perimeters from the descriptions can be more of a challenge.

Name _____

Date _____

Find the perimeter of the square.

4.25cm

Find the perimeter of the rectangle.

2.7cm

6.6cm

What is the perimeter of a square with sides of 3.25cm?

What is the perimeter of a square with sides of 5.9cm?

A square has a perimeter of 24cm. What is the length of each side?

A square has a perimeter of 30cm. What is the length of each side?

A square has a perimeter of 13cm. What is the length of each side?

What is the perimeter of a rectangle with sides of 6.25cm and 3.25cm?

A rectangle has a perimeter of 20cm. One of the sides is 7cm long. What are the lengths of the other sides?

A rectangle has a perimeter of 26cm. One of the sides is 8cm long. What are the lengths of the other sides?

A rectangle has a perimeter of 30cm. One of the sides is 4.6cm long. What are the lengths of the other sides?

Teacher's notes

Ensure that the pupils understand that the perimeter is the total distance around a shape. Finding missing lengths using other known facts is particularly challenging.

Andrew Brodie: Improving Problem-solving Skills for ages 9-10 © Bloomsbury Publishing Plc 2013

Bus timetable

The timetable shows the times of buses from Ringdown to Payton.

	Bus A	Bus B	Bus C	Bus D
Ringdown	0915	1004	1139	1346
Sports Centre	0925	1014	1149	1356
Railway Station	0935	1024	1159	1406
Garden Centre	0940	1029	1204	1411
Payton	0952	1041	1216	1423

Teacher's notes

Discuss the bus timetable, ensuring that the pupils can interpret the times shown. Ask questions such as: How long does it take for a bus to get from Ringdown to the Sports Centre? How long from the Sports Centre to the Railway Station? How long from Ringdown all the way to Payton?

Bus timetable

Name _____

Date _____

Look at the timetable showing the times of buses from Ringdown to Payton.

At what time does Bus B leave Ringdown?

Now give your last answer in 12-hour clock notation.

How long does it take Bus A to get from Ringdown to the Sports Centre?

Do all of the buses take the same amount of time for the journey from Ringdown to the Sports Centre?

How much time does it take for Bus A to travel from the Sports Centre to the Railway Station?

For how many minutes is Bus A travelling from the Railway Station to the Garden Centre?

How many minutes long is the journey from the Garden Centre to Payton?

For how long will you be travelling if you catch the bus in Ringdown and go all the way to Payton?

If you get on the 1159 bus at the Railway Station, at what time will you reach Payton?

If you leave the Sports Centre at 1356, at what time will you reach the Garden Centre?

Now give your last answer in 12-hour clock notation.

Teacher's notes

Give the children a copy of the bus timetable. Help them to interpret the questions. Are they confident in the use of am and pm to show 12-hour clock times?

Andrew Brodie: Improving Problem-solving Skills for ages 9-10 © Bloomsbury Publishing Plc 2013

Name _____

Date _____

Look at the timetable showing the times of buses from Ringdown to Payton.

At what time does Bus C leave Ringdown?

Now give your last answer in 12-hour clock notation.

At what time does the 1024 bus from the Railway Station reach Payton?

Now give your last answer in 12-hour clock notation.

How much later does Bus B leave Ringdown than Bus A?

How much later does Bus C leave Ringdown than Bus A?

How much later does Bus D leave Ringdown than Bus A?

Bus E leaves Ringdown at 1558. It takes the same amount of time over each part of the journey as the other buses. Complete the timetable for Bus E.

	Bus A	Bus B	Bus C	Bus D	Bus E
Ringdown	0915	1004	1139	1346	
Sports Centre	0925	1014	1149	1356	
Railway Station	0935	1024	1159	1406	
Garden Centre	0940	1029	1204	1411	
Payton	0952	1041	1216	1423	

Teacher's notes

Give the children a copy of the bus timetable. Help them to interpret the questions. Are they confident in the use of am and pm to show 12-hour clock times?

Bus timetable

Name _____

Date _____

Look at the timetable showing the times of buses from Ringdown to Payton.

At what time does the 1149 bus from the Sports Centre
reach Payton?

Now give your last answer in 12-hour clock notation.

Bus E arrives at Payton at 4.35pm and Bus F leaves Ringdown at 6.26pm. Both buses take the same amount of time over each part of the journey as the other buses. Complete the timetable for Buses E and F.

	Bus A	Bus B	Bus C	Bus D	Bus E	Bus F
Ringdown	0915	1004	1139	1346		
Sports Centre	0925	1014	1149	1356		
Railway Station	0935	1024	1159	1406		
Garden Centre	0940	1029	1204	1411		
Payton	0952	1041	1216	1423		

How much later does Bus F leave Ringdown than Bus A?

Erica needs to be at a meeting at the Garden Centre at 4.30pm.
Which bus should she catch from Ringdown to arrive on time
for her meeting?

Sid arrives at Ringdown at 11.52am. How long does he
have to wait for the next bus?

Each bus takes an average time of 2 minutes to cover each
kilometre in distance. What is the speed of
the bus in kilometres per hour?

Approximately how many kilometres is it
from Ringdown to the Sports Centre?

Approximately how many kilometres is it
from Ringdown to Payton?

Teacher's notes

Give the children a copy of the bus timetable. Help them to interpret the questions. Are they confident in the use of am and pm to show 12-hour clock times? You may need to discuss the speed questions with them: some children find it helpful to 'scale up' when considering speed. For example, if it takes 2 minutes to cover 1km, how far would be covered in 10 minutes? The answer to this question can now be used to find out how far would be covered in 1 hour - this shows the average speed of the bus.

Andrew Brodie: Improving Problem-solving Skills for ages 9-10 © Bloomsbury Publishing Plc 2013

Sports kits

football shorts

football shirt

football socks

netball shirt

netball skirt

netball bib

Item	Price
football shorts	£6.74
football shirt	£8.07
football socks	£5
netball skirt	£8.95
netball shirt	£6.50
netball bib	£3.15

Teacher's notes

Talk about the prices of the items. How much would it cost to buy a complete kit for football? How much for a complete kit for netball? How much for a complete kit for a football team of 11 players? For a netball team of 7 players?

Sports kits

Name _____

Date _____

Item	Price
football shorts	£6.74
football shirt	£8.07
football socks	£5
netball skirt	£8.95
netball shirt	£6.50
netball bib	£3.15

How much more is a netball skirt than a pair of shorts for football?

How much would it cost to buy a shirt and shorts for football?

What would be the total cost of a pair of socks and a shirt for football?

What would be the total cost of all three items for football?

How much would it cost to buy a shirt and skirt for netball?

What would be the total cost of a bib and a shirt for netball?

What would be the total cost of all three items for netball?

Which is more expensive, all three football items or all three netball items?

How much more expensive?

Teacher's notes

Talk about the prices of the items. Ensure that the pupils can read and understand the questions. The penultimate question will need solving in stages.

Andrew Brodie: Improving Problem-solving Skills for ages 9-10 © Bloomsbury Publishing Plc 2013

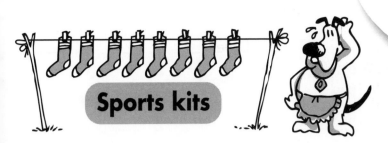

Sports kits

Complete the chart to show the prices for 10 of each item.

Item	Price	Price for 10 items
football shorts	£6.74	
football shirt	£8.07	
football socks	£5	
netball skirt	£8.95	
netball shirt	£6.50	
netball bib	£3.15	

How much more is a football shirt than a netball shirt? |_____|

How much would it cost to buy 5 football shorts and 5 netball skirts? |_____|

How much would it cost to buy 5 football shirts and 5 netball shirts? |_____|

How much would it cost to buy 15 football shorts and 15 netball skirts? |_____|

How much would it cost to buy 15 football shirts and 15 netball shirts? |_____|

How much would it cost to buy all three items for a complete team of 11 football players? |_____|

How much would it cost to buy all three items for a complete team of 7 netball players? |_____|

How much more expensive is it to buy the kit for the football team than for the netball team? |_____|

Teacher's notes

Talk about the prices of the items. Ensure that the pupils can read and understand the questions. Can they make use of the prices they have entered in the third column of the table to find the costs of 5 items and of 15 items?

Name _____

Date _____

Complete the chart to show the prices for 10 of each items and the price with a 30% discount.

Item	Price	Price for 10 items	30% discount price for bundle of 10 items
football shorts	£6.74		
football shirt	£8.07		
football socks	£5		
netball skirt	£8.95		
netball shirt	£6.50		
netball bib	£3.15		

The school PE teacher wants to buy 11 of each football items.
What is the cheapest total cost of 11 pairs of football shorts?

What is the cheapest total cost of 11 football shirts?

How much would the school save by buying all three items for the
11 members of the football team at the discount price
compared to the full price?

The school PE teacher wants to buy enough netball skirts for all 7 members of the netball team. She can't decide whether to buy 10 skirts to take advantage of the discount or just to buy the 7 skirts she needs. Use the space below to investigate and compare the costs then write what you would do and why.

Teacher's notes

Talk about the prices of the items. Ensure that the pupils can read and understand the questions. Can they make use of the prices they have entered in the third column of the table to find the discount prices?

Andrew Brodie: Improving Problem-solving Skills for ages 9-10 © Bloomsbury Publishing Plc 2013

Cornflake cakes

Ingredients you will need to make 8 cornflake cakes:

110g cooking chocolate

70g raisins

2 tablespoons golden syrup

50g butter

60g cornflakes

Teacher's notes

Talk about the ingredients, explaining that the recipe itself is not shown but simply the amounts. Ideally pupils could weigh out some of the ingredients to gain awareness of quantities. Should you wish to go ahead and make the cakes: melt the cooking chocolate, butter and syrup and stir the mixture; mix the raisins and cornflakes then combine it with the chocolate mixture; share into 8 cake cases and leave the cakes to set in a cool place.

Cornflake cakes

Ingredients you will need to make 8 cornflake cakes:

> **110g cooking chocolate**
>
> **70g raisins**
>
> **2 tablespoons golden syrup**
>
> **50g butter**
>
> **60g cornflakes**

What weight of chocolate would be needed to make just 4 cakes instead of 8?

What weight of raisins would be needed to make 4 cakes instead of 8?

How much golden syrup would be needed to make 4 cakes instead of 8?

What weight of butter would be needed to make 4 cakes instead of 8?

What weight of cornflakes would be needed to make 4 cakes instead of 8?

What weight of chocolate would be needed to make 16 cakes?

What weight of raisins would be needed to make 16 cakes?

How much golden syrup would be needed to make 16 cakes?

What weight of butter would be needed to make 16 cakes?

What weight of cornflakes would be needed to make 16 cakes?

Teacher's notes
Ensure that the pupils understand that the abbreviation 'g' represents grams. Can they use halving skills to find the amounts for 4 cakes? Do they notice that they could find the amounts for 16 cakes by doubling the amounts for 8 or by multiplying the amounts for 4 by 4?

Andrew Brodie: Improving Problem-solving Skills for ages 9-10 © Bloomsbury Publishing Plc 2013

Cornflake cakes

Ingredients you will need to make 8 cornflake cakes:

110g cooking chocolate

70g raisins

2 tablespoons golden syrup

50g butter

60g cornflakes

What weight of chocolate would be needed to make 12 cakes?

What weight of raisins would be needed to make 12 cakes?

How much golden syrup would be needed to make 12 cakes?

What weight of butter would be needed to make 12 cakes?

What weight of cornflakes would be needed to make 12 cakes?

What weight of chocolate would be needed to make 20 cakes?

What weight of raisins would be needed to make 20 cakes?

How much golden syrup would be needed to make 20 cakes?

What weight of butter would be needed to make 20 cakes?

What weight of cornflakes would be needed to make 20 cakes?

Teacher's notes

Ensure that the pupils understand that the abbreviation 'g' represents grams. Many children find these problems difficult but encourage them to look at the relationship between 8 and 12: if they halve the amounts for 8 to find the amounts for 4 they can then either add the amounts for 8 and 4 together or they can multiply the amounts for 4 by 3.

Cornflake cakes

Ingredients you will need to make 8 cornflake cakes:

> **110g cooking chocolate**
>
> **70g raisins**
>
> **2 tablespoons golden syrup**
>
> **50g butter**
>
> **60g cornflakes**

What weight of chocolate would be needed to make 24 cakes? ▢

What weight of raisins would be needed to make 24 cakes? ▢

How much golden syrup would be needed to make 24 cakes? ▢

What weight of butter would be needed to make 24 cakes? ▢

What weight of cornflakes would be needed to make 24 cakes? ▢

What weight of chocolate would be needed to make 36 cakes? ▢

What weight of raisins would be needed to make 36 cakes? ▢

How much golden syrup would be needed to make 36 cakes ▢

What weight of butter would be needed to make 36 cakes? ▢

What weight of cornflakes would be needed to make 36 cakes? ▢

Teacher's notes

Ensure that the pupils understand that the abbreviation 'g' represents grams. Many children find these problems difficult but encourage them to look at the relationship between 8 and 24: they can simply multiply by 3. But how do the pupils find the amounts for 36? There are several ways this can be done – ask them to explain the methods they used.

Andrew Brodie: Improving Problem-solving Skills for ages 9-10 © Bloomsbury Publishing Plc 2013